CHAKRA
HEALING JOURNAL

A Guided Journal to
Help You Balance Your
Chakras for Health
and Positive Energy

MICHELLE JOEUSON

CASTLE POINT BOOKS
NEW YORK

www.castlepointbooks.com

The Castle Point Books trademark is owned by Castle Point Publishing, LLC.
Castle Point books are published and distributed by St. Martin's Publishing Group.

ISBN 978-1-250-27387-1 (trade paperback)

Our books may be purchased in bulk for promotional, educational, or business use.
Please contact your local bookseller or the Macmillan Corporate and Premium Sales
Department at 1-800-221-7945, extension 5442, or by email at
MacmillanSpecialMarkets@macmillan.com.

Design by Melissa Gerber
Images used under license by Shutterstock.com

First Edition: 2021

10 9 8 7 6 5 4 3 2 1

JOURNAL YOUR WAY TO
CHAKRA HEALING!

You are a unique rainbow of energy; a crucial link in a universal network of cosmic power. Running from the base of your spine to the top of your head are your seven major chakras, or energy centers, laid out like a roadmap to enlightenment. Ancient Hindu and Buddhist teachings reveal that these individual vortexes of energy hold the secrets to finding strength, love, security, and inspiration within and around us. When they are blocked or closed, we cannot find comfort or balance in our lives. Putting unexpressed emotions on the pages of this journal can help open those chakras so that we can feel whole and at peace.

Spend a few quiet moments every day releasing emotions connected to each of the seven major chakras and working toward a new level of physical, mental, and spiritual wellness. Let this journal be your soul's companion as you strive to harness and balance the energy within and find your way to personal fulfillment.

MAKE TIME to consider the energy flowing through you. Tune into your subtle body, the current of life force that flows within. If you need to sit quietly or meditate to do so, feel free. Describe how well or balanced you feel in these three realms:

PHYSICAL BODY
(tired or energized, ill or strong)

_____

_____

_____

_____

_____

_____

_____

_____

_____

_____

_____

_____

MIND

(dominated by negative or positive thoughts)

_____

_____

_____

_____

_____

_____

_____

SPIRIT

(inspired or uninspired)

_____

_____

_____

_____

_____

_____

_____

ROOT CHAKRA

SAFETY, SECURITY, GROUNDING

LOCATE THE ROOT CHAKRA at the base of your spine. This is your survival chakra; the seat of your needs both physical (shelter, food, water, etc.) and non-physical (understanding, belonging, etc.). Take a moment to close your eyes and tune in by taking deep breaths and focusing on the base of your tailbone. Notice any resistance as you inhale and exhale, and breathe more deeply into this space. When you're ready, answer the prompt below.

What do you need to feel supported, connected, and understood?

_____

_____

_____

_____

_____

How can you get these needs met?

_____

_____

_____

_____

Use the mantra below to summon feelings of strength and security:

**I have the power and capacity to find
support in people, places, and things.**

The root chakra is tied to the earth element, so healing is facilitated by spending quality time with the earth.

Take yourself on a date with nature (without your phone), even if it's only for five minutes. Write about your experience with nature below.

_____

_____

_____

_____

How can you weave some therapeutic nature time into your daily life?

_____

_____

_____

_____

Your root chakra functions as a sturdy foundation providing a sense of safety and sureness that allows you to plant your feet firmly in the ground. How confident, safe, and grounded do you feel?

_____

_____

_____

_____

_____

_____

_____

Whenever your unsteadiness or insecurities set you off balance, make time to return to the earth and reflect on the feelings it stirs or quiets in you.

The root chakra is associated with our capacity to trust in the Universe, to truly feel that we are supported in our lives, and to know that our needs can be met.

Notice ways in which you have resisted trusting in the unknowns of your life.

_____

_____

_____

_____

_____

How can you begin to build more trust with your relationship to the Universe?

_____

_____

_____

_____

_____

The universe has my back.

—GABRIELLE BERNSTEIN

The root chakra is the headquarters of your insecurity, some of which may be financial. Release any unexpressed emotions surrounding money and financial security. You may not be able to change your financial status, but confronting these emotions is key to unlocking the root chakra. What worries do you have about money, if any?

_____

_____

_____

_____

_____

_____

_____

_____

_____

_____

_____

_____

Signs of an imbalanced
root chakra: negativity,
fear, greed, paranoia

The root chakra is our foundational chakra. This foundation can either be strong or weak, depending on how stable and secure we are in all areas of our life.

What are some areas of your life (physical, emotional, mental, spiritual, financial, family, or other) that are satisfyingly stable?

_____

_____

_____

_____

_____

_____

What makes them so secure?

_____

_____

_____

_____

_____

Is there any area of your life that could use more stability?

_____

_____

_____

_____

_____

_____

How would achieving stability in this area of your life bring you more fulfillment and security?

_____

_____

_____

_____

_____

_____

_____

Inner stability creates a strong foundation for our other chakra centers to function properly and flow.

Our root chakra is connected to our generational patterns. This means that we tend to take on both positive and negative patterns from our parents, which our parents inherited from their parents, and so on.

What positive and negative patterns have you inherited from your parents?

_____

_____

_____

_____

_____

How might these patterns affect your life and way of being?

_____

_____

_____

_____

_____

_____

_____

Sound vibrations are thought to be part of our life energy. Use sound therapy and the Bija mantras from the Vedic tradition to align the root chakra. Each major chakra has a Bija mantra associated with it. From a seated or lying-down position, chant the word Lam (pronounced Lum) over and over to yourself to clear energy blockages in the root chakra. Allow the powerful vibration of that word to work its healing. Describe the experience below.

Create a more personal mantra for yourself that helps summon your courage. Think or say it when you need to balance out feelings of fear or insecurity. Choose from the ones below or create your own.

I am stronger and braver than I know.

My feet are firmly planted.

I have all the strength I need.

The power of the universe lies within me.

_____

_____

_____

_____

_____

_____

_____

_____

Hold a stone in your hand or place it on the root chakra point to facilitate the flow of energy. Hematite and red jasper are both good options when unlocking the root chakra.

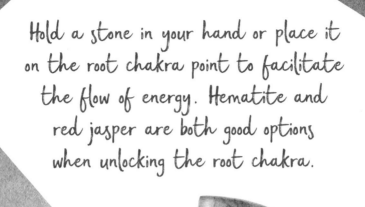

Red Jasper

Hematite

Each of the major chakras is associated with a color. The root chakra is red, conveying confidence and courage. To build on this energy, consider adding more red to your life.

Make a list of your favorite red foods, red clothing, and red objects that can help clear blockages in the root chakra.

_____

_____

_____

_____

_____

_____

_____

_____

_____

_____

_____

_____

Too much red in your life can bring feelings of anger or irritability.

SACRAL CHAKRA

EMOTIONS, SENSATIONS, PLEASURE

LOCATE THE SACRAL CHAKRA, which is situated approximately three fingers' width below the navel. This is your emotional center where your sensations are held and expressed. Take a moment to close your eyes and tune in, taking deep breaths and focusing on your lower abdomen. Pay attention to any sensations that you feel. When you're ready, answer the prompts below.

How healthy is my relationship with my emotions?

_____

_____

_____

_____

Do I allow myself to express them freely and without judgment?

_____

_____

_____

_____

_____

Check in with yourself today and consider how well you tune into your emotions and whether you allow yourself to feel what you're feeling. Use the mantras below to activate the sacral chakra and invite healing:

I honor the spectrum of my emotions.

My emotions are messengers that help me recognize what thoughts, feelings, and beliefs are no longer serving me.

My awareness of these triggers enables me to heal them and integrate more wholeness in order to experience emotions that do serve me.

The sacral chakra is tied to the water element, so a powerful way to heal this chakra is by spending time in or around water.

How do you most often commune with water?

_____

_____

_____

_____

_____

_____

An easy way to commune with water every day is to imagine water cleansing you as you drink it, wash your face, wash your hands, shower, or take a bath. Imagine that it is cleansing you, washing away all that no longer serves you, and nourishing every cell in your body.

Because our sacral chakra is connected to water, it reminds us to be in a state of flow. Our emotions can be seen as the currents that create movement, stillness, and waves within the water.

How do you perceive your waters to be flowing within you right now? Describe those currents below.

_____

_____

_____

_____

_____

_____

_____

_____

_____

The water element represents life, receptivity, fertility; emotions, healing, and purity.

Because the sacral chakra is our emotional center, when it is imbalanced it can be difficult to feel or can cause emotional imbalances. To bring it back into alignment, it's important to connect with your feelings by connecting with your sensations (sight, smell, taste, touch, and hearing).

How often do you tap into your senses?

_____

_____

_____

_____

_____

_____

_____

_____

_____

_____

_____

_____

_____

_____

Brainstorm ways you can be more present with your sensations. For example, eating a meal and paying attention to the different tastes and smells or closing your eyes for a few minutes and listening to the different sounds around you.

_____

_____

_____

_____

_____

_____

Set aside time for a sensual "date" sometime this week to do one of the items on your brainstorm list. Return to your list every week or so to make future sensual dates.

The sacral chakra is our pleasure center. Pleasure isn't just sexual, it's also about doing things that we simply enjoy doing.

What activities, hobbies, and experiences bring you pleasure?

_____

_____

_____

_____

_____

_____

_____

How can you invite more of these activities, hobbies, and experiences into your life?

_____

_____

_____

_____

_____

How easy is it for you to treat yourself to the things you love most? If you notice any guilt or shame for doing pleasurable things, write about it below. Ask yourself why you haven't allowed yourself to enjoy these things. Next time you are about to do something that brings you pleasure, give yourself full permission to enjoy it.

Signs of an imbalanced sacral chakra: emotional imbalance, addiction, shame, and guilt.

Sexuality is one expression of our uniqueness and creativity. It is a powerful and inspiring energy we can tune into. Think about your relationship to your sexuality.

Do you feel free to express yourself sexually?

_____

_____

_____

_____

_____

When does your sexuality make you feel empowered, inspired, and more at peace?

_____

_____

_____

_____

_____

_____

There is deep wisdom
within our very flesh,
if we can only come to
our senses and feel it.

—ELIZABETH A. BEHNKE

Hold a stone in your hand or place it on the location of your sacral chakra to facilitate the flow of energy. Orange and gold-colored stones like citrine can help unlock your sacral chakra.

Citrine

Being playful and incorporating play is a great way to balance the sacral chakra. It keeps you light in your heart and body and enables your creativity to flow freely. All of us (yes, even adults) need play and a recess from all of the seriousness of life.

What are ways you can be more playful in your life?

_____

_____

_____

_____

_____

_____

_____

_____

_____

_____

_____

_____

Use sound therapy and the Bija mantras from the Vedic tradition to align your sacral chakra. Each major chakra has a Bija mantra associated with it. From a seated or lying-down position, chant the word Vam (pronounced Vum) repeatedly to yourself to clear energy blockages in the sacral chakra. Allow the powerful vibration of Vam to work its healing. Describe the experience below.

_____

_____

_____

_____

_____

_____

_____

_____

_____

_____

Adopt a personal mantra to awaken your sacral chakra. Choose from the ones below or create your own. Think or say your chosen mantra out loud whenever you want to balance this chakra.

I am full of passion and life force energy.

I honor all of my emotions and express them in healthy ways.

I give myself permission to feel and experience pleasure.

I am a sensual creative being.

Each of the major chakras is associated with a color. The sacral chakra is orange, conveying passion and pleasure. To build upon this energy, consider adding more orange to your life.

Make a list of your favorite orange foods, orange clothing, and orange objects that can help open the sacral chakra.

_____

_____

_____

_____

_____

_____

_____

_____

_____

_____

_____

_____

_____

SOLAR PLEXUS CHAKRA

IDENTITY, CONFIDENCE, WILLPOWER

LOCATE THE SOLAR PLEXUS CHAKRA, which is situated approximately three fingers' width above the navel. This is your center of identity and ego where your personal power and confidence originates. Take a moment to close your eyes and tune in, taking deep breaths and focusing on your upper abdomen. When you're ready, answer the prompts below.

What does the word confidence look like and feel like to you?

_____

_____

_____

_____

_____

What's your favorite way to boost your confidence?

_____

_____

_____

_____

_____

_____

Confidence is less about how you appear to others, and more about owning who you are and radiating from that place of authentic expression. It's not focused on the thoughts of others, but rather knowing the value of one's self. It magnetizes and inspires purely through one's embodiment.

What is one of the many values you bring to the world?

_____

_____

_____

_____

_____

_____

_____

_____

_____

_____

_____

_____

The solar plexus is associated with the fire element. Close your eyes and imagine that there's a flame located in your solar plexus. As you take deep breaths, imagine this flame increasing, growing larger and more vibrant. Visualize it expanding outward until it surrounds your whole body. Imagine this fire burning away all of your insecurities, doubts, and limiting beliefs. Write down your experience below.

What was burned away? What are you happy to have released?

_____

_____

_____

_____

_____

_____

_____

_____

_____

_____

Fire symbolizes rebirth, passion, action, power, and transformation.

The solar plexus chakra is all about our personal power. Make a list of all the things that make you feel empowered and happy. This list could include a color, an activity, an article of clothing, a genre of music—anything!

Use this list as a personal reference and tool to boost your mood and align with your power.

_____

_____

_____

_____

_____

_____

_____

_____

_____

_____

_____

Manipura is the original Sanskrit name for the solar plexus, which means "shining gem."

Confidence is closely linked with our beliefs surrounding our identity and self-worth. It's the outward expression of our self-esteem. How we view ourselves dictates how we think, feel, and behave.

What beliefs about yourself are you holding on to, even though they are no longer serving you? Write about them below.

_____

_____

_____

_____

_____

How can you reword these beliefs or create brand-new ones that empower you? Write them below!

_____

_____

_____

_____

_____

_____

_____

If the fire in your heart
is strong enough, it will
burn away any obstacles
that come your way.

—SUZY KASSEM

The solar plexus loves when you take risks, but only the type that you want to take.

What are some things that you want to do that scare you? Write them down and explain why they excite or frighten you.

_____

_____

_____

_____

_____

_____

_____

_____

_____

_____

_____

_____

_____

_____

How would it feel to actually go after those things that excite or frighten you? Reflect on how your confidence and quality of life could change as a result.

List three positive changes in your life that could come from taking such risks.

_____

_____

_____

_____

_____

_____

_____

_____

_____

_____

_____

_____

_____

_____

Our solar plexus can fall out of alignment when we are not living with personal integrity.

Take a moment to reflect on whether there is an area of your life in which you are not abiding by your own rules.
Why do you feel this way?

_____

_____

_____

_____

_____

_____

_____

_____

_____

_____

_____

_____

What principles do you live by, or want to live by, that will help you regain or maintain your sense of personal integrity?

_____

_____

_____

_____

_____

_____

_____

_____

_____

_____

_____

Signs of an imbalanced solar plexus chakra: anxiety, low self-esteem and confidence, inertia, controlling behavior, and a weak sense of self.

Physical movement is one simple way to activate this chakra. Next time you are doing one of these activities or exercises, imagine that your solar plexus is being recharged like a battery.

Write down a list of all your favorite ways to move your body.

_____

_____

_____

_____

_____

_____

_____

_____

_____

_____

_____

The solar plexus converts inertia into movement, ideas into action, and dreams into reality.

Take a walk outside today. While you are walking, have a goal in mind that you want to achieve. As you take each step, imagine that you are moving one step closer toward that goal and really feel the emotions as if it were real. You can also imagine that with each step, you are becoming more you, or coming into your power or confidence. Write about your experience below.

The solar plexus asks that we take full responsibility for our lives and accountability for our choices, which is when true empowerment begins. Take a moment to be radically honest with yourself and where you are at in your life. Are you living a life that brings you fulfillment and joy?

_____

_____

_____

_____

_____

_____

What needs to change or be realigned in your life?

_____

_____

_____

_____

_____

_____

Hold tiger's eye
in your hand or place it
on the location of your solar plexus
chakra to facilitate more healing!

Tiger's Eye

Use sound therapy and the Bija mantras from the Vedic tradition to align your solar plexus chakra. Each major chakra has a Bija mantra associated with it. From a seated or lying-down position, chant the word Ram (pronounced Rum) repeatedly to yourself to clear energy blockages located in your solar plexus chakra. Allow the powerful vibration of Ram to work its healing. Describe the experience below.

_____

_____

_____

_____

_____

_____

_____

_____

_____

_____

_____

_____

_____

_____

Adopt a personal mantra to use to awaken your solar plexus chakra! Think or say this mantra out loud whenever you want to feel more in balance. Choose from the ones below or create your own.

I align with the truth of who I am.

I confidently show up in my authentic expression.

I move forward with confidence and integrity.

I make choices that make me feel empowered.

Each of the major chakras is associated with a color. The solar plexus chakra is yellow, conveying confidence and willpower. To build upon this energy, consider adding more yellow to your life.

Make a list of your favorite yellow foods, yellow clothing, and yellow objects that can help to activate your solar plexus chakra.

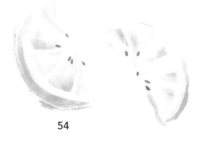

Add some lemon to your water to activate its life force and open your solar plexus chakra!

HEART CHAKRA

LOVE, COMPASSION, BEAUTY

LOCATE THE HEART CHAKRA, which is situated in the center of your chest. This is your love center from which compassion and kindness radiate. Take a moment to close your eyes and tune in, taking deep breaths and focusing on the center of your chest. Anytime your mind starts to chatter, drop down your focus into the heart and continue taking deep breaths. When you're ready, answer the prompts below.

How connected do you feel to your heart and its wisdom?

_____

_____

_____

_____

_____

Does it have any messages for you at this moment?

_____

_____

_____

_____

_____

Hold a stone in your hand
or place it on the location of
your heart chakra to facilitate
the flow of energy. Rose quartz and
malachite are both good options
when unlocking your heart chakra.

Rose Quartz

Malachite

The heart chakra is associated with the air element. A powerful way to activate this chakra is by taking deep conscious breaths. Take a moment to take some deep breaths from your heart space. Visualize your heart expanding with each breath. Imagine that with each breath, you are creating more space for love to flow in. Write about your experience below.

The heart chakra opens whenever we feel and express gratitude. This is why practicing gratitude is known to welcome more feelings of joy and appreciation. What are you grateful for in your life right now?

Kindness originates from the heart chakra. Kindness brings a warmth to not only your heart chakra, but to all of those around you. This warmth enables the heart chakra to activate and open.

What is one act of kindness that you can do for someone else today?

_____

_____

_____

_____

_____

Recall and describe an act of kindness someone else did for you. How did it make you feel?

_____

_____

_____

_____

_____

Criticism, bitterness, and judgment (of self and others) closes the heart chakra. Kindness opens the heart chakra.

When your heart chakra is open, you can give and receive love. Consider whether your heart chakra is open. Think about your current relationships: Do you feel comfortable giving in your relationships? Why or why not?

_____

_____

_____

_____

_____

_____

Do you feel comfortable receiving in your relationships? Why or why not?

_____

_____

_____

_____

_____

_____

_____

When your heart
speaks, take
good notes.

—JUDITH CAMPBELL

Self-love is one of the most powerful prescriptions for healing our heart chakras. Take a moment to love and honor yourself by writing down some things you love about yourself below.

_____

_____

_____

_____

_____

_____

_____

_____

_____

_____

_____

_____

_____

_____

_____

What are some of your favorite self-love practices and rituals? If you don't have any, write down ones that you would like to start doing below.

_____

_____

_____

_____

_____

_____

_____

_____

_____

_____

_____

_____

_____

_____

_____

_____

_____

Working with your inner child is a great way to heal and open your heart chakra. Think about your younger self. If it helps, find a picture of your younger self to inspire reflection.

What would you say to your younger self if he or she were standing in front of you right now?

_____

_____

_____

_____

_____

What do you think he or she needs to hear right now?

_____

_____

_____

_____

_____

What would your younger self say to you if he/she could see where you are now?

_____

_____

_____

_____

_____

_____

_____

_____

_____

_____

_____

_____

_____

_____

Let's begin to cultivate a relationship with your inner child! What are some activities and things that you enjoyed doing as a little kid? Make a list below.

Rediscovering childish delights and adding them back into your life will keep you young and light in spirit, and keep your heart chakra open.

How can you reintroduce some of these activities from the previous page into your life today?

_____

_____

_____

_____

_____

_____

_____

_____

_____

_____

_____

_____

_____

_____

_____

Take a moment to check in with your heart, noting any sorrow within it. If you are holding onto any anger, guilt, resentment, or pain from the past, write about it below.

_____

_____

_____

_____

_____

_____

_____

_____

How can you let go of the past?

_____

_____

_____

_____

_____

_____

Holding onto past pains and losses closes our heart chakra and sometimes even causes resentment. Letting go opens our heart chakra.

Use sound therapy and the Bija mantras from the Vedic tradition to align your heart chakra. Each major chakra has a Bija mantra associated with it. From a seated or lying-down position, chant the word Yam (pronounced Yum) repeatedly to yourself to clear energy blockages located in your heart chakra. Allow the powerful vibration of Yam to work its healing. Describe the experience below.

_____

_____

_____

_____

_____

_____

_____

_____

_____

_____

_____

_____

_____

Adopt a personal mantra to help awaken your heart chakra! Think or say this mantra out loud whenever you want to balance this chakra. Choose from the ones below or create your own.

I choose love.

I am full of love and kindness.

I am compassionate towards myself and others.

I am grateful for everything in my life.

Each of the major chakras is associated with a color. The heart chakra is green, conveying love and healing. To build upon this energy, consider adding more green to your life.

Make a list of your favorite green foods, green clothing, and green objects that can help open your heart chakra.

THROAT
CHAKRA

COMMUNICATION, TRUTH, INTEGRITY

LOCATE THE THROAT CHAKRA,
which is situated at the base of your neck in
the hollow spot where your collar bones meet.
This is your communication center from which
you express your truth. Take a moment to close
your eyes and tune in, taking deep breaths and
focusing on the base of your neck. Keep taking
these deep breaths to create that connection.
When you're ready, answer the prompts below.

Do you feel confident when expressing your thoughts, ideas, and feelings?

_____

_____

_____

_____

Why or why not?

_____

_____

_____

_____

_____

Sodalite

Hold a stone in your hand or place it on the location of the throat chakra to facilitate the flow of energy. Sodalite and lapis lazuli are both good options when opening your throat chakra.

Lapis Lazuli

Your throat chakra is the space from which you speak It is the space that is created for your truth to be expressed. Imagine filling this space with your desired intention before you speak. For example, you might fill that space with love before you speak loving words. Consider an intention that you have; something you want to manifest in your life. Write down some intentions below. Make space for one of these intentions in your throat chakra, then speak it out loud.

Spaciousness gives you more peace and freedom in your day-to-day life. We all accumulate clutter in our minds, homes, and schedules.

Which, if any, feels cluttered today?

_____

_____

_____

_____

_____

What helps you clear your mind?

_____

_____

_____

_____

_____

The throat chakra is associated with the ether element. Ether means "space" or "spaciousness."

The throat chakra activates when you use your voice. Find new ways to use your voice, whether that's singing, screaming into a pillow, humming your favorite song, laughing, sighing, making unusual noises, or playing around by sounding out different tones. Try to express how you're feeling with sounds.

What are some fun new ways you can use your voice to express yourself?

_____

_____

_____

_____

_____

_____

_____

_____

_____

_____

_____

_____

Close your eyes and imagine a bright blue light where your throat chakra is. Imagine it spinning clockwise, increasing in speed as you take deep breaths, and purifying your throat chakra. Draw or describe your experience below.

Your personal truth is subjective to you and only you. Others can only guide you toward, or remind you of, what is already true for you.

What truths define you and the way you want to live your life?

_____

_____

_____

_____

_____

_____

What "untruths" are you ready to let go of?

_____

_____

_____

_____

_____

_____

_____

_____

Surrendering to who you really
are and why you are here may
very well change the world.

—MARIA FLYNN

The way you speak to yourself and about yourself is a reflection of what you believe to be true about yourself. Shifting the way in which you speak to or about yourself will help you gain an awareness that can redirect your life in a good way. Think about the quality of your inner thoughts. How do you speak to yourself?

_____

_____

_____

_____

_____

_____

_____

_____

_____

_____

_____

_____

_____

_____

How do you speak to others?

_____

_____

_____

_____

_____

_____

_____

_____

_____

How can you speak more kindly to yourself and about yourself
to others?

_____

_____

_____

_____

_____

Compliments are a great way to use your throat chakra in a loving way. Write down three compliments about yourself below, then say them out loud. For even more good vibes, write down three more compliments you'd like to give to friends, family members, or coworkers. Be sure to verbalize them the next time you see them in person.

_____

_____

_____

_____

_____

_____

_____

_____

_____

_____

_____

_____

_____

_____

Think about the complaints you have voiced lately. Get in the habit of shifting those thoughts into what you can be grateful for in this moment.

Write down three recent complaints you thought or made below. Then, rewrite them as positives or words of gratitude.

Complaining is a misuse of the throat chakra's energy and weaken it

Nonverbal communication is how you speak to others without words. Take a moment to notice your posture, eye contact, body language, and facial expressions the next time you communicate with others.

How well do you communicate your feelings without words?

_____

_____

_____

_____

_____

_____

_____

_____

_____

_____

_____

Mindfulness is a great way to become aware of your inner thoughts.

The throat chakra isn't just about speaking but knowing when to listen. Listening creates spaciousness (ether) between moments of expression and opens us up to both giving and receiving. Ways to listen: listen to others, listen to your own inner voice, and listen to nature.

What did you, or do you, hear today?

_____

_____

_____

_____

_____

_____

_____

_____

_____

_____

_____

_____

Use sound therapy and the Bija mantras from the Vedic tradition to align your throat chakra. Each major chakra has a Bija mantra associated with it. From a seated or lying-down position, chant the word Ham (pronounced Hum) repeatedly to yourself to clear energy blockages in your throat chakra. Allow the powerful vibration of Ham to work its healing. Describe the experience below.

Adopt a personal mantra for you to use to awaken your throat chakra! Think or say this mantra out loud whenever you want to balance this chakra. Choose from the ones below or create your own.

I lovingly speak my truth.

I freely and confidently express who I am.

I live in integrity with my personal truth.

I use my words to speak kindly of myself and others.

Each of the major chakras is associated with a color. The throat chakra is blue, conveying integrity and truth. To build upon this energy, consider adding more blue to your life.

Make a list of your favorite blue foods, blue clothing, and blue objects that can help open your throat chakra.

THIRD EYE CHAKRA

PERCEPTION, IMAGINATION, INTUITION

LOCATE THE THIRD EYE CHAKRA,
which is situated in the center of your forehead
above your eyebrows. This is your center of
perception where imagination and intuition are
housed. Take a moment to close your eyes and
tune in, taking deep breaths and focusing on the
center above your eyebrows. When you're ready,
answer the prompts below.

Do you trust your intuition?

_____

_____

_____

_____

_____

How can you begin to work with or trust your intuition more?

_____

_____

_____

_____

_____

_____

Moonstone

Hold a stone in your hand or place it on the location of the third eye chakra to facilitate the flow of energy. Moonstone and labradorite are both good options when working with your third eye chakra.

Labradorite

The third eye chakra is associated with the element of light. A great exercise for activating this chakra is candle gazing meditation. Light a candle and set a timer for three minutes. As you gaze into the candle, imagine the flame clearing and opening your third eye chakra. Write about your experience below.

_____

_____

_____

_____

_____

_____

_____

_____

_____

_____

_____

_____

Stargazing is also a great activity for activating the third eye chakra.

Imagine a vibrant indigo light entering your third eye chakra. Imagine it breaking through any walls within your mind, purifying your perception. Visualize the light clearing any heavy energies within your mind and thoughts that no longer serve you. Write about your experience below.

The light element symbolizes truth, wisdom, enlightenment, and love.

The third eye chakra is the door to our imagination. It wants us to use our imagination to envision possibilities.

What do you envision for your life? Allow your imagination to run wild on this page.

Worrying and expecting the worst
is a misuse of your imagination.
Use your imagination to focus and
create more of what you do want!

Because the third eye chakra is all about perception, it's important to consider how we perceive ourselves, life, and the world around us.

How do you perceive yourself? How do you perceive your life? Describe it in detail.

_____

_____

_____

_____

_____

_____

_____

_____

_____

_____

_____

_____

_____

How do you perceive the state of the world around you?

_____

_____

_____

_____

_____

_____

_____

_____

_____

_____

_____

_____

Signs of an imbalanced third eye chakra: rigid
perspectives, paranoia, disillusion, a lack of clarity,
headaches, and close-minded thinking.

The third eye chakra loves to gain different perspectives so it can expand our minds into new ways of thinking. How open are you to new and different perspectives?

_____

_____

_____

_____

_____

_____

_____

_____

_____

_____

_____

_____

_____

_____

Think of each perspective that challenges your own as an opportunity to gain deeper insights.

When have your ideas been challenged recently?

_____

_____

_____

_____

_____

_____

How did you handle it?

_____

_____

_____

_____

_____

_____

_____

Learning new things is a great way to not only expand our skills and deepen our understanding, but also to open up our minds. Write down a list of things that you are interested in learning more about here.

_____

_____

_____

_____

_____

_____

Make a second list here of things you are willing to try.

_____

_____

_____

_____

_____

_____

_____

To be creative means to
be in love with life.

—OSHO

Use sound therapy and the Bija mantras from the Vedic tradition
to align your third eye chakra. Each major chakra has a Bija mantra
associated with it. From a seated or lying-down position, chant the
word U (pronounced Ooo) repeatedly to yourself to clear energy
blockages in your third eye chakra. Allow the powerful vibration of U to
work its healing. Describe the experience below.

_____

_____

_____

_____

_____

_____

_____

_____

_____

_____

_____

_____

_____

Adopt a personal mantra to awaken your third eye chakra! Think or say this mantra out loud whenever you want to balance this chakra. Choose from the ones below or create your own.

I trust that my intuition is always guiding me.

I use my imagination to envision the possibilities for my life.

I am open to new ways of thinking.

I am willing to try and learn new things.

Each of the major chakras is associated with a color. The third eye chakra is purple, conveying wisdom and intuition. To build upon this energy, consider adding more purple to your life.

Make a list of your favorite purple foods, purple clothing, and purple objects that can help open your third eye chakra.

CROWN
CHAKRA

HIGHER SOURCE, ONENESS, INSPIRATION

LOCATE THE CROWN CHAKRA, which is situated at the crown of your head. This is your center of connection to a higher source where you experience oneness and inspiration. Take a moment to close your eyes and tune in, taking deep breaths and focusing on the top of your head. When you're ready, answer the prompts below.

Do you believe in a higher source?

_____

_____

_____

_____

_____

If so, what is your way of connecting to that higher source, or how would you like to begin connecting?

_____

_____

_____

_____

_____

Hold a stone in your hand or place
it on the location of your crown chakra to
facilitate the flow of energy. Amethyst
and clear quartz are both good options
when working with this chakra.

The crown chakra allows you to view the bigger picture in your life. It helps to align you with what's truly important and to redirect your energy. Take a moment to zoom out and view the bigger picture of your life right now.

Using this perspective, what no longer matters as much to you?

_____

_____

_____

_____

_____

_____

_____

_____

How can you redirect your energy to support the bigger picture in your life? Note any goals that have changed by incorporating this perspective.

_____

_____

_____

_____

_____

_____

_____

_____

_____

_____

_____

_____

_____

_____

_____

_____

When you feel connected to a higher source, you realize that life is always trying to teach you something. Even during hardships, there is a lesson. Take a moment to reflect on your life right now.

What life lessons have you experienced and grown from?

_____

_____

_____

_____

_____

What are the lessons that life is currently trying to teach you?

_____

_____

_____

_____

_____

_____

And suddenly you
realize: you are in every
dot of the universe
vanishing and arising.

—AMIT RAY

When we feel connected to life and everything in it, we feel a sense of wholeness and oneness. Some people feel most connected when they are out in nature, running, or spending time with their children. Take a moment to consider when you feel most connected. When and how does this feeling of connection happen for you?

Take a moment to close your eyes, taking deep breaths from your crown chakra. Visualize a white light entering your crown chakra and moving through your whole chakra system. Imagine that as you take deep breaths, it is cleansing, balancing, and activating all of your chakras. Imagine your crown chakra opening more with each breath to enable more white light to pour in. Write about your experience below.

Prayer of any form is a great way to activate the crown chakra. Speaking to a higher source creates a sacred space and opens the channel for us to connect with the Universe. Set aside personal time when you can express your deepest wishes, goals, desires, fears, sorrows, and gratitude to your higher source. What is something you want to pray for right now? Write it below.

Posture can help us find peace and balance. Savasana, or laying face up, palms up in "corpse pose" can help unblock the crown chakra.

Think of your crown chakra as your spiritual Wi-Fi connecting you to the Universe. If you have a weak connection, you can strengthen it by building your trust and faith.

How can you have more faith in your journey and process?

_____

_____

_____

_____

_____

_____

_____

_____

_____

_____

_____

_____

_____

When you have an opened crown chakra, there is a feeling of oneness with all of life and nature. It's a deep inner knowing that all of life is connected.

Have you ever experienced this feeling of oneness?

_____

_____

_____

_____

_____

_____

How can you welcome this feeling into your life?

_____

_____

_____

_____

_____

_____

The crown chakra is where inspiration originates. Inspiration stimulates your soul to create. Who inspires you?

_____

_____

_____

_____

_____

_____

_____

_____

_____

_____

_____

_____

_____

_____

_____

What has inspired and continues to inspire you most in your life?

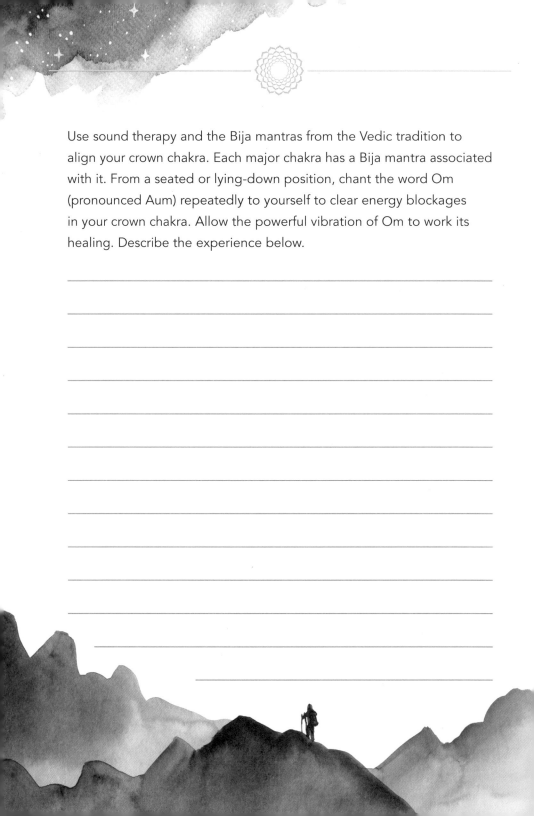

Use sound therapy and the Bija mantras from the Vedic tradition to align your crown chakra. Each major chakra has a Bija mantra associated with it. From a seated or lying-down position, chant the word Om (pronounced Aum) repeatedly to yourself to clear energy blockages in your crown chakra. Allow the powerful vibration of Om to work its healing. Describe the experience below.

_____

_____

_____

_____

_____

_____

_____

_____

_____

_____

_____

_____

Adopt a personal mantra for you to awaken your crown chakra. Think or say this mantra out loud whenever you want to balance this chakra. Choose from the ones below or create your own.

I am at one with everything in the Universe.

I am inspired to create a life I love.

I trust my journey and have faith in the process.

I see the bigger picture in my life.

Take care of yourself every day and find ways to open your chakras and keep the positive energy flowing. Make time to meditate, reflect, and journal when any of your chakras feel depleted, overactive, or blocked. Use this page as a daily reminder of the beautiful rainbow within you.

CROWN CHAKRA: INSPIRATION AND CONNECTION

CROWN CHAKRA: INTUITION

THROAT CHAKRA: COMMUNICATION

HEART CHAKRA: LOVE

SOLAR PLEXUS CHAKRA: CONFIDENCE

SACRAL CHAKRA: EMOTIONS

ROOT CHAKRA: SECURITY